I0813582

# AIRCRAFT CARRIERS

John Willis

www.openlightbox.com

**Step 1**
Go to **www.openlightbox.com**

**Step 2**
Enter this unique code
**KEVLWLKEG**

**Step 3**
Explore your interactive eBook!

MEGA MILITARY MACHINES

AV2

# AIRCRAFT CARRIERS

Start!

Share

AV2 is optimized for use on any device

## Your interactive eBook comes with...

**Audio**
Listen to the entire book read aloud

**Videos**
Watch informative video clips

**Weblinks**
Gain additional information for research

**Try This!**
Complete activities and hands-on experiments

**Key Words**
Study vocabulary, and complete a matching word activity

**Quizzes**
Test your knowledge

**Slideshows**
View images and captions

**Share**
Share titles within your Learning Management System (LMS) or Library Circulation System

**Citation**
Create bibliographical references following APA, CMOS, and MLA styles

**This title is part of our AV2 digital subscription**


**1-Year K–5 Subscription**
**ISBN** 978-1-7911-3320-7


Access hundreds of AV2 titles with our digital subscription.
Sign up for a FREE trial at **www.openlightbox.com/trial**

The digital components of this book are guaranteed to stay active for at least five years from the date of publication.

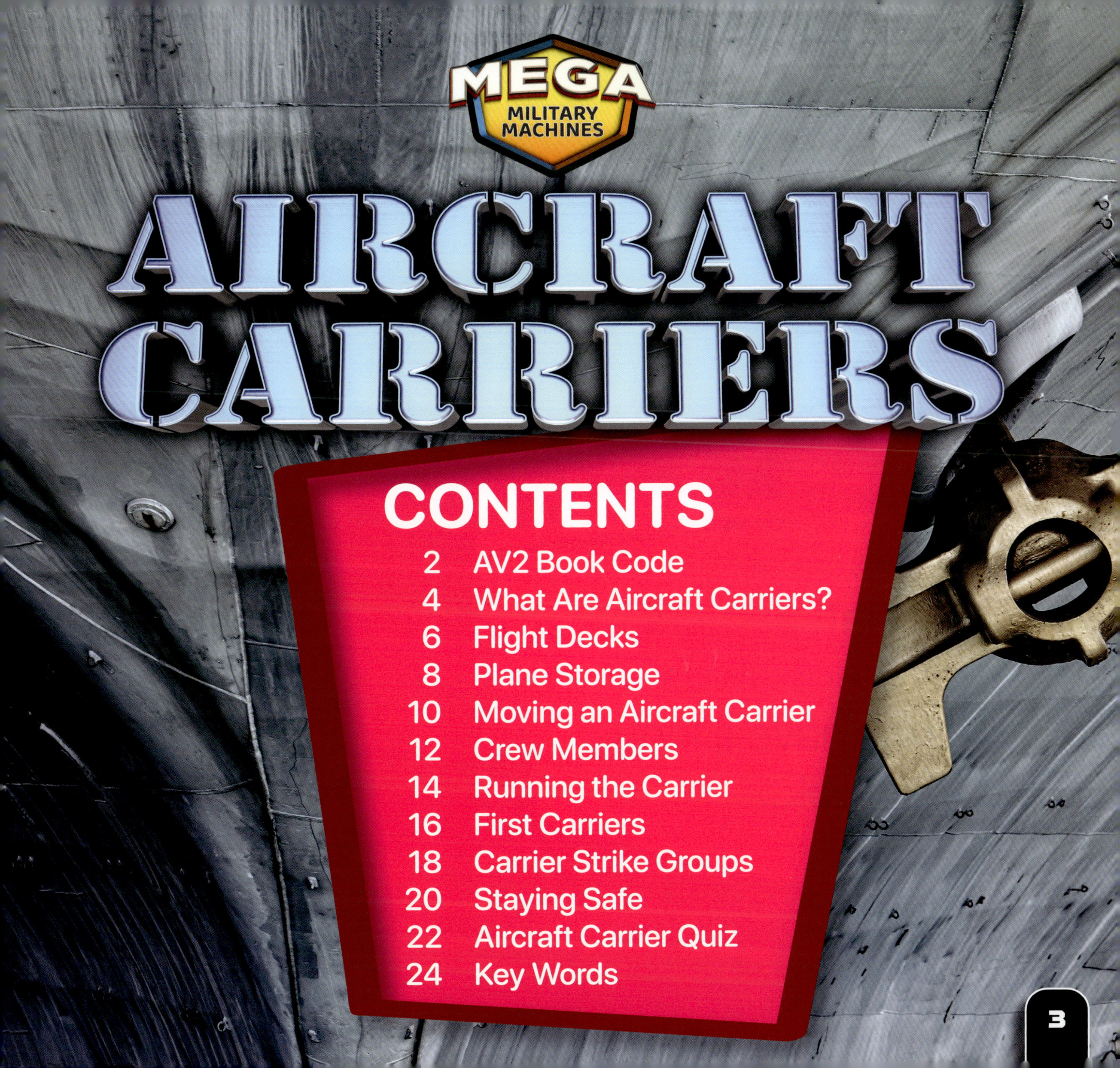


# AIRCRAFT CARRIERS

## CONTENTS

Aircraft carriers are huge ships. They have a long, flat deck.

COMPARING LENGTHS
School Bus
About **35 feet** (10 meters)
Airplane
About **225 feet** (70 m)
Aircraft Carrier Runway
About **500 feet** (150 m)

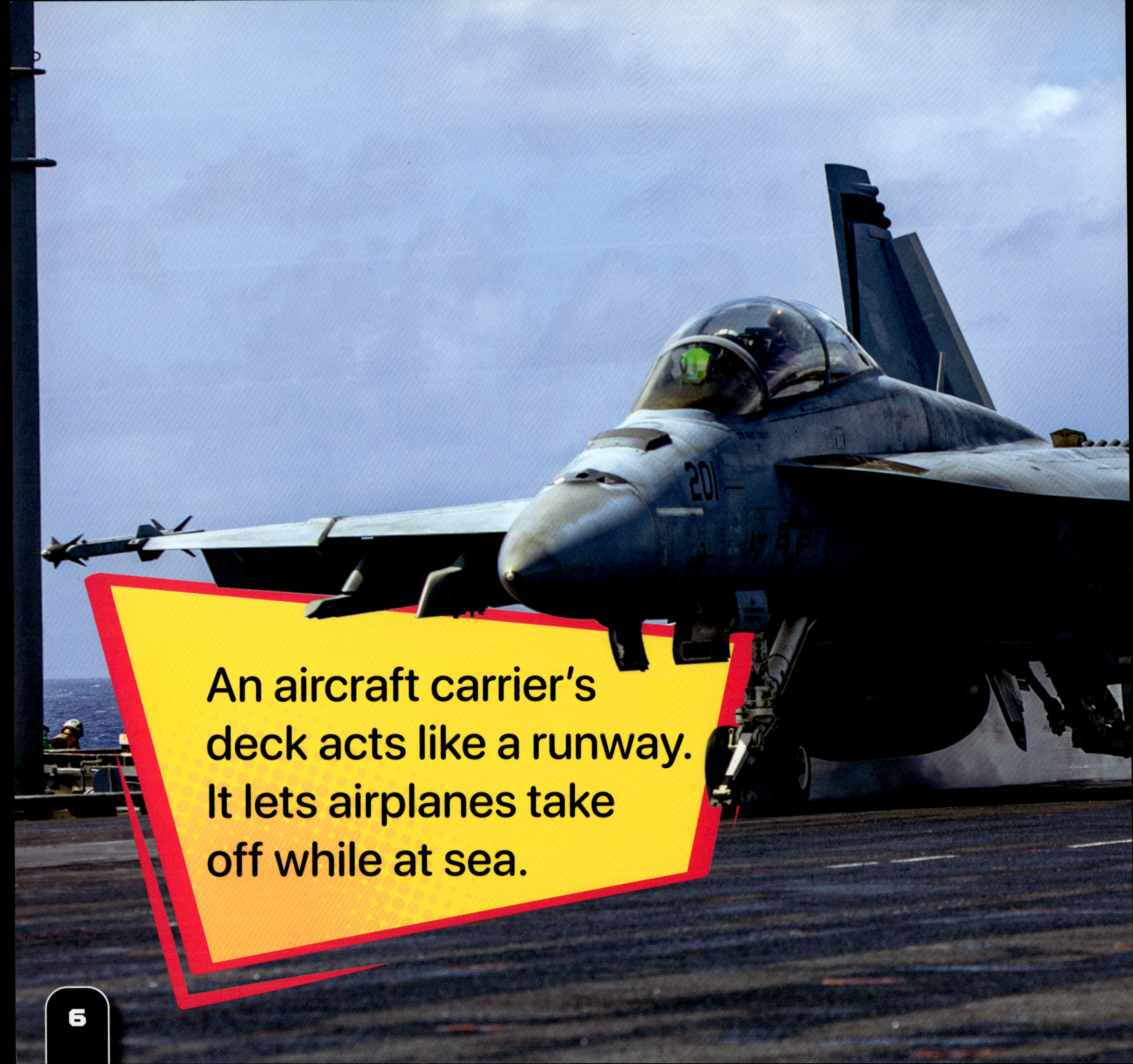

An aircraft carrier's deck acts like a runway. It lets airplanes take off while at sea.

Some decks have catapults to help planes speed up when they take off.

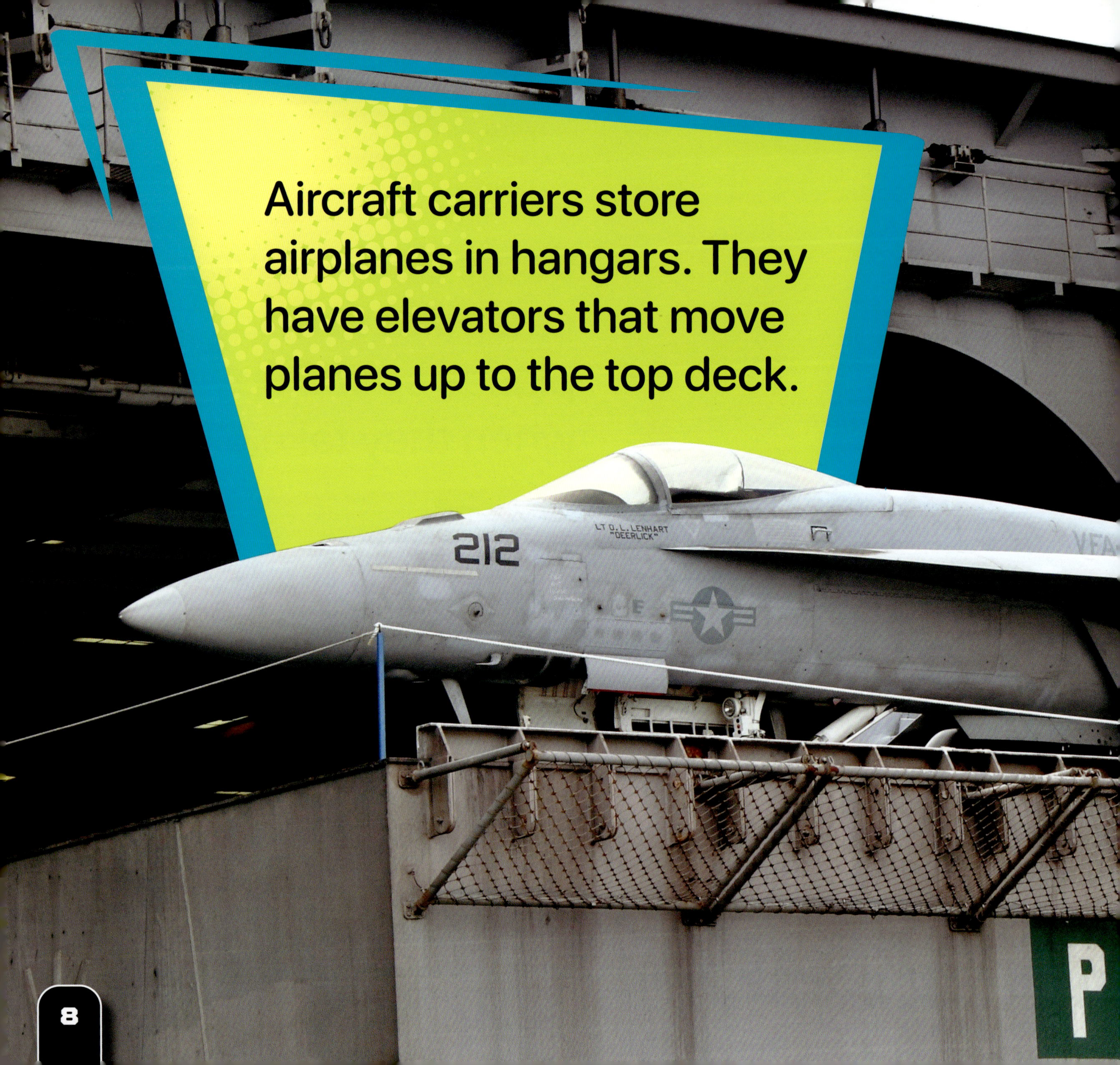


Aircraft carriers store airplanes in hangars. They have elevators that move planes up to the top deck.

9
P

Aircraft carriers use large propellers to move. The propellers spin to push the ship through the water.

**COMPARING SPEEDS**

**Bicycle**

About **15 miles per hour** (25 kilometers per hour)

**Aircraft Carrier**

About **35 miles per hour** (55 kmph)

**Airplane**

About **580 miles per hour** (930 kmph)

The propellers can move the carrier forward or backward.

Aircraft carriers are like floating cities. They have crews made up of thousands of sailors and pilots.

BEWARE OF JET BLAST
PROPELLERS AND ROTORS

The person in charge of the carrier is called the captain. The captain controls the carrier from a large tower called the island.

ISLAND
The island is about 150 feet (46 m) tall.

The first aircraft carrier used by the United States Navy was called the USS *Langley*. It operated more than 100 years ago.

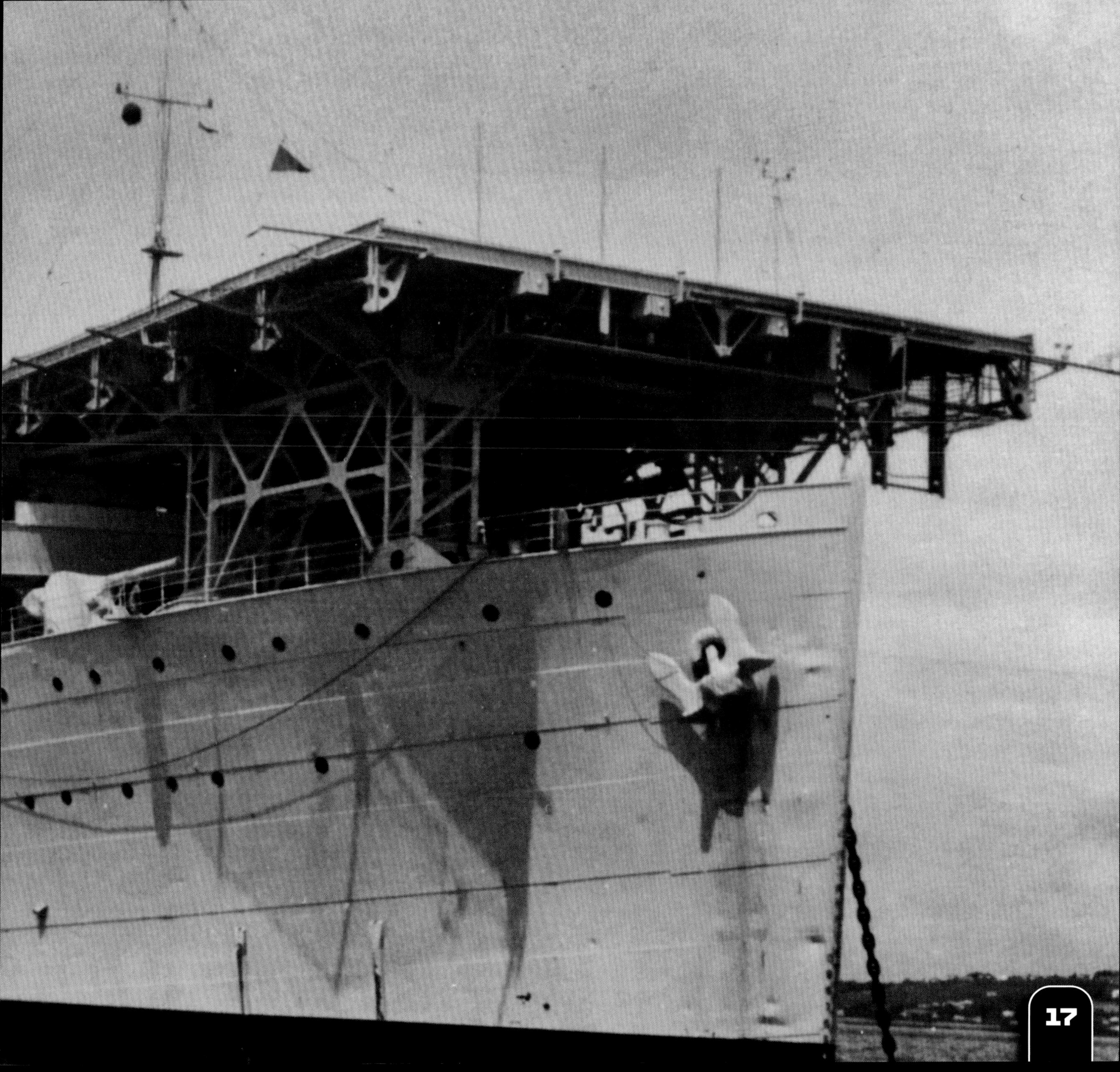

Carriers work with other ships. Together they make up a carrier strike group.

**WHAT IS IN A CARRIER STRIKE GROUP?**

1 Aircraft Carrier + 2 Guided Missile Cruisers + 2 Anti-Aircraft Warships + 2 Anti-Submarine Destroyers or Frigates

Destroyers, cruisers, and frigates can be part of a carrier strike group. Their job is to protect the carrier.

Working on an aircraft carrier can be dangerous. Carriers have many tools to keep the large crew safe.

**See what you have learned about aircraft carriers.**

Which of these pictures does not show an aircraft carrier?
2020498-S
3
82AB 107
212
P
9

# KEY WORDS

Research has shown that as much as 65 percent of all written material published in English is made up of 300 words. These 300 words cannot be taught using pictures or learned by sounding them out. They must be recognized by sight. This book contains 58 common sight words to help young readers improve their reading fluency and comprehension. This book also teaches young readers several important content words, such as proper nouns. These words are paired with pictures to aid in learning and improve understanding.

| Page | Sight Words First Appearance |
|---|---|
| 4 | a, are, have, long, they |
| 5 | about, feet, school |
| 6 | an, at, it, lets, like, off, sea, take, while |
| 7 | help, some, to, up, when |
| 8 | in, move, that, the |
| 10 | large, miles, through, use, water |
| 11 | can, or |
| 12 | and, made, of |
| 14 | from, is |
| 16 | by, first, more, states, than, was, years |
| 18 | group, make, other, together, what, with, work |
| 19 | be, part, their |
| 21 | keep, many, on |

| Page | Content Words First Appearance |
|---|---|
| 4 | aircraft carriers, deck, ships |
| 5 | airplane, lengths, runway, bus |
| 7 | catapults |
| 8 | elevators, hangars |
| 10 | bicycle, propellers, speeds |
| 12 | cities, crews, pilots, sailors |
| 14 | captain, island, person, tower |
| 16 | Navy, USS *Langley* |
| 18 | anti-aircraft warships, anti-submarine destroyers, anti-submarine frigates, carrier strike group, guided missile cruisers |
| 19 | job |
| 21 | tools |

Published by Lightbox Learning Inc.
276 5th Avenue, Suite 704 #917
New York, NY 10001
Website: www.openlightbox.com

Copyright ©2024 Lightbox Learning Inc.
All rights reserved. No part of this publication may be reproduced, stored in a retrieval system, or transmitted in any form or by any means, electronic, mechanical, photocopying, recording, or otherwise, without the prior written permission of the publisher.

Library of Congress Control Number: 2023931793

ISBN 978-1-7911-5530-8 (hardcover)
ISBN 978-1-7911-5531-5 (softcover)
ISBN 978-1-7911-5532-2 (multi-user eBook)

Printed in Guangzhou, China
1 2 3 4 5 6 7 8 9 0 27 26 25 24 23

042023
100922

**Project Coordinator:** Priyanka Das **Designer:** Terry Paulhus

Every reasonable effort has been made to trace ownership and to obtain permission to reprint copyright material. The publisher would be pleased to have any errors or omissions brought to its attention so that they may be corrected in subsequent printings.

The publisher acknowledges Alamy, Dreamstime, Getty Images, Shutterstock, the U.S. Navy, and Wikimedia as the primary image suppliers for this title.